AT THE TENT OF HEAVEN
by
Philip St. Clair

Ahsahta Press

Boise State University
Boise, Idaho

Some of these poems first appeared in the following magazines and anthologies: ***Chandrabhaga, Hiram Poetry Review, Kencompotl, Maybe Mombasa, New Kent Quarterly, Night House Anthology*** (Four Zoas Night House Ltd.), ***Nightsun, Perspectives on a Grafted Tree*** (Perspectives Press), ***Pudding, Shelley's, Uroboros, Visions,*** and ***Winter***. Others are forthcoming in ***Live Writers***.

Special thanks are due to Murray Bowes, Sanford Marovitz, and David St. Clair for their support and advice.

Editor for Ahsahta Press: Tom Trusky

PS
3569
T12
.A94

ISBN 0-916272-24-9

Library of Congress Catalog Card Number:
83-072317

to the memory of my father

Contents

Introduction

By the time that Philip St. Clair brought out his first collection of poetry in 1980, **In the Thirty-Nine Steps**, he had already begun the series of poems that would evolve into his next one, which is **At the Tent of Heaven**. The difference between the two volumes is vast. Each of the earlier poems is entirely discrete, and as a whole the collection reveals a sense of the poet's detachment reflected through tightly controlled syntax, abundant mechanistic imagery, and visions of death. **At the Tent of Heaven**, in contrast, is a unified series of verbal portraits in a language that is spare yet vital with color and movement, plain yet dignified by the discipline of the prosody and the oral approach of the poet, whose sympathy for his Native American subject matter is always evident but never obtrusive.

St. Clair attributes this sympathy in part to a presumed Shawnee element in his own background, which he has traced to his great-great-grandmother, who lived in Columbiana County, Ohio during the 1850s. Her grandson, the poet's grandfather—with "skin the color of a copper penny"—has long remained at the edge of his imagination, "a shadow figure," as St. Clair calls him. But until the past few years this haunting presence in his background had not yet coalesced in his imagination with his creative energy as a poet. The two elements merged through his position as an editor in the late 1970s with Volair Ltd., a small but highly artistic publisher of expensive, limited-edition books.

One of the Volair volumes he edited was **History of the Indian Tribes of North America**, by Thomas L. McKenney and James Hall, a three-volume compilation of hand-colored lithograph portraits and accompanying biographical texts from the late 1830s. In writing **At the Tent of Heaven**, St. Clair has turned back to the McKenney and Hall volumes as his principal source for biographical information on the twenty-two subjects of his poem-portraits. Among these he has interpolated a second series of poems on the single figure of Red Jacket to add both a unifying chronological thread and an alternate perspective. Meant to embody "traditional Iroquois values and the decline of their power," according to St. Clair, the figure of Red Jacket is developed more fully than that of any other in the collection. As a result he may be regarded as the center to which a reader constantly returns from wide-ranging explorations among many other tribes of his generation, both east and west of the Mississippi. Furthermore, seeing Red Jacket's life pass from childhood through the age of nobility and heroism to his imminent death adds poignancy to his brief "biography" and deftly touches with melancholy the emerging composite portrait of the passing heroes, cowards, and loved ones being described.

The twenty-two portraits have been arranged, St. Clair says, "to represent displacement by the whites, the persistence and continuation of Native beliefs, and an ultimate spiritual transcendence." Although each of the figures has been drawn from the McKenney and Hall volumes, few are individuals of major historical consequence. Instead, St. Clair has focused upon tangential figures of both sexes, whose lives attracted his attention by virtue of the complex of moral circumstances which confronted them. It has been his aim not to depict the ideal, as McKenney had attempted in his lithographs, or to assert the heroic over other human qualities, but rather to disclose those universalities by which the Native American of from one and a half to two centuries ago can be related to, instead of distinguished from, contemporary readers. Consequently, he may depict the cowardice of a son as a balance to the heroism of a mother ("Totapia"), one spokesman's drunkenness ("Metea") as a balance to another's austerity and discipline ("Little Crow"), the treachery of a Creek chief ("McIntosh") as a balance to the tribal loyalty of a Dacotah ("Notchimine").

St. Clair is at times astonishing in the depth of character he can reveal through relatively few lines. He describes his figures effectively without recourse to abundant detail; instead, he employs a few specifics and nuances tellingly—as in referring briefly to a quiet spearfisherman's dream of ornamentation glittering upon him as he dances ("Caa-Tou-See") and to the blue beads driven into the neck of a captive maiden by her captors before they are slain by her father ("Oshegwun"). Although his forte is narration, he insists that he has no intention of "retelling history" or dealing anthropologically with his materials. But just as the Native American sources have provided him with what he calls "an armature," a skeletal structure upon which to build his poetry, so does the element of *story* enable him to convey the human truths he wishes to impart.

Neither idealizing nor propagandizing, Philip St. Clair has thoughtfully heeded Charles Olson's advice to find the universal in the local, and he has consequently enabled us to acquire a deeper, richer understanding of our essential relation to the original inhabitants of America through the medium and art of poetry than even the most sympathetic historian or propagandist can provide. *At the Tent of Heaven* testifies to the strength and originality of his new poetic voice.

Sanford E. Marovitz
Kent, Ohio
September, 1983

AT THE TENT OF HEAVEN

Have ye not known? Have ye not heard? Hath it not been told to you from the beginning? Have ye not understood from the foundations of the earth?

It is he that sitteth upon the circle of the earth . . . that stretcheth out the heavens as a curtain, and spreadeth them out as a tent to dwell in:

That bringeth the princes to nothing; he maketh the judges of the earth as vanity.

Isaiah

Ah-Wey-Ne-Yonh

The mother of Red Jacket
May 1782

Before my son could run, he swam.
Brown fishes, wedges in water,
Held his eyes. His babyhood
Passed in gazing the river.

Freed from the cradleboard
He crawled near the riveredge,
Scrabbling up bright pebbles
As I snatched him back.

He gave one me! He pressed it
In my hand. Then with my mind
I named him Took-Up-Stone,
Being vain in what to give him.

Since then, that name has lived in silence:
I work away at quiet magic.
Often my tongue would move to speak:
I hold it still to flesh the thinking.

1

Moanahonga

An Ioway Warrior
August 1824

To survive the stigma of his humble birth
Envy became defense: those who were higher
He ignored or avoided. He was surly,
Morose—an exile since the womb.

He was given proud lips. He had taken
Many wives. His eyelids always rode tense.
He made a call for people to come:
Some did. His followers called him

Big Neck and permitted a chieftainship
Because of his strength in a fight.
They lived apart, alone. His enemies,
Who all outranked him, called him Great Walker.

Soon he felt strong enough to join hands
With others. He made treaties. His first act
Was to witness a cession of millions of acres
For five thousand dollars.

                      He wept once only
When a message came from the land he sold:
The Whites had tumbled his parents
From the stiltings of their faceless repose
To plough them through the rich, dark ground.

Wakawn

A Winnebago Chief
December 1834

At the knife's point since peace, for he liked
The whites, and was curious to hear them
Talking. This gave him quarrels
With chiefs to the north and northwest:
Once, under a beech tree,
He had to speak with his life
Dancing in the air before his lips.

He was the first at Prairie du Chien to turn
Their way. He asked to be taught to plow,
And when he learned he threw aside the blanket
To gather and stoop by his wife.

The superintendent, who needed all of him,
Said, Snake, Christ says He is a Brother
Yet you show Him the back of your head.
He wants you to ask Him for ponies and blankets.
He wants you to live within Him. Try.
When you pray in the lodge, He weeps blood.

Snake said, My children have listened
Because I tell them to.
White hands are always moving. Whites are
Never without food; that is good in these times.
For me, I am too old, and old men weary
Of young men gifting. I have sang
Over much ground. I have been much too free.

Ah-Wey-Ne-Yonh

to her sisters
September 1762

They found him hiding in a den of rocks.
He was too weak to bare his teeth
When our men took him from his bed of leaves.
His soft brown hair was heavy with dirt.
Each fevered, trembling, freckled cheek
Was scarred from tears.

                          His eyes
Frightened me: blue eyes, wolf's eyes,
Eyes wide and hard from being alone.
I grew cold when he stared at me: I knew
White people are greedy, crazy. I knew
They strike their children.

                          But I took him,
That little lost one, and washed him in the river,
And dressed him, and fed him from the kettle,
And placed him among my sons, and I smiled at him
When he pleased me, and when he angered me
My tongue had edges.

                          That was all I did.
Now he grows and is strong, and he runs
With my own, and his pale legs flash
As birches among pines, and his eyes
Are warm and soft when I look in them,
For he is whole.

                    Sisters!
When he asks me why he came to be here
This is what my heart tells me to say:
Spirit touched us long ago in dream-time,
Little owl, and when winds blew you from your nest
You came to me.

Little Crow
A Dacotah Chief
April 1833

In the first spring past peace, King George
Called all his allies among Nations:
Drummond's Island shone with bright muskets,
And there were many bolts of cloth. But Crow
Cursed him by saying, These are empty mirrors
From empty men. For you we fought a people
We did not know, and now you have peace,
And now we have none. Tell us—what do we
With the great new neighbor who hates us?
Now you are not speaking—I will take nothing.

He fell away from the breath of his people
To the shores of the Great Lake. He was reduced
To the hunting of beaver. No one would talk
On what he had done, or whether he had done it,
For he was Kahpozhay, a Son of Light,
And in his loins grew all the true seed
Of the Sioux and Dacotah:
As he and his son rode north for wisdom,
All villages saluted his blood.
Chiefs held his horse and called him Father.

Quatawapea

A Shawnoe Chief
January 1807

Because he was the best-dressed delegate
In the small, stuffy, candlelit annex
To the large reception hall, the Secretary
Draped him with an oval medal. His forehead,
Strong jawline, firm chin were impressive
To the Secretary, who had once read a tract
On physiognomy.

        That image of Jefferson,
Struck in silver, glanced out of the blue
Of his jacket: on his return to the Ohio
He had listeners, for a very strong man
Had lifted him over the others
To set him down honored. On that evening
His words rose up with the councilfire.

Soon after that the people did not listen.
They smiled and spoke him with respect
But did not listen. There were others
Whose words were too wise, whose faces
Were not as comely. He thought on this,
And when the medal he wore turned black,
He polished it with soft wood ashes.

Red Jacket

solus
May 1774

Maple-seeds are falling. Wind
Clacks them together over my head.
I think on good noises.
I think on turtle-rattles.

As they float they make circles
And buttons of gold. They land
On their faces. Their mouths
Embrace the earth in a life

Of one breath. Their bodies
Stand straight in tall grass.
They are plumes of gold
That address heaven.

I am a man. I am a seed.
The Great League's will
Slants my path as I fall
From the womb, and I try

All motions of grace as I rush
To the earth, and my daughters
Will be strong trees whose branches
Bear heavy in spring.

I am a man who craves children.
I think on good noises
And dancing in circles
To the sound of turtle-rattles.

Oshegwun

A Chippewa Woman
April 1778

Before she could marry, the Sioux
Raided her hunting party and killed many.
Caught up in panic, she ran, she was taken,
And her captors lashed her to an oak.

The two young braves were at odds: each
Wanted her, so they locked arms
And fought as bears for her.

Those men were too well matched: they came
Near death, and bitter sweat
Ran over their bloody teeth.

Helping the other up, they drew knives
And slashed her free. They stood by her,
Saying, Choose between me and me.

Through them she ran at the forest.
A blunt club wheeled the air
And struck her back: she fell

To the little dark. Then the braves
Lost respect: each scalped one side.
Their knives drove blue beads in her neck.

When she awoke, she saw both were dead:
Her father, with two muskets, had followed her.
She lived to bear nine sons, one daughter,
And the beads in her throat never came out.

The Wives of Red Jacket

Black-Bead-Woman
August 1774

This day is hot. Beetles and blackflies
Drone in the village. My husband is away,
Being a husband, talking to allies and
Brothers.

        I go to the river for water.
The wooden pail is heavy. Heavier
When it is full. The other women are fat
And ugly. They tire me. Their mouths spill over
With children.

        Water, water,
Show my face to me. Show me
My hair, my black hair caught in braids,
My black hair captured by ribbon and brass
To flash at the eyes of young men.
Show me large eyes that trouble dreams
On breezeless nights in summer,
When many are restless in the loins
And cannot sleep.

        Dream-time, dream-time,
Show me openings in the forest, where
Tiny blue flowers scatter as stars. There,
Dressed in snow-white buckskin, heavy
With beadwork, I will lie down,
And when I rise, tiny sky-blossoms
Will dapple my garment, and when I dance
Young men will play the flute to me forever.

Clasp-Of-Silver
May 1779

Where the low places are, hidden in valleys
Near the places for the drawing of water,
Trilliums stand on the cool hills.
The shade is a mantle for their faces.

I walk among their whiteness, seeking the one
With a countenance of blue fire: the one
I dream of in the good days of False Faces
When we heal each other by laughter.

Each spring I find him. Each spring
I am sad, for the edges of his petals
Are brown and gnarled. He nods to me
In his affliction, and I remember my dreams.

I kneel to cradle his face in my hands.
I blow the gentle breath of healing.
I make a mask to let him laugh:
I twist my mouth; I cross my eyes.

For the blue flower of my heart is given
Over my lips, down through my hands.
My breasts are blue. My nipples are blue.
I ache with the fullness of blue milk.

Kishkalwa

A Shawnoe Chief
May 1802

The Dark and Bloody Ground lay south
Of the Ohio, where the buffalo
Drank up strong rivers, and game sprang
At every footfall: here the hungry enemy
Was thick, and no one tribe spoke.

Since he kept a young man's heart, he left
To trick the men he hunted with:
He would become a living bush
And slow-walk them as the sky turned red.

But five of the enemy saw him: a shot
Cut his ear, and as he ran the grapevines
Reached at him, and runt trees
Caught all his clothes and his weapons.

His return was hard; there was grinning; who
But a puppy would cast everything aside
To run faster, and who is this young man
Who gives enemies good trophies?

His words meant nothing, for the tale
Made his Brothers wink to his back.
No coward walks upon this Ground, he said.
Dress me, arm me, let me flesh out.

He left the camp alone. The next day
He came at them with two fresh scalps.
They laughed a long time. Feed me, he said.
Let me have ten men who fight.

He came back with the ten who followed him
And twenty scalps. This is still the boy,
They said, who showed us his naked rump.
Go kill the trees that took your clothes.

Then give me thirty and let the Ground
Feast, he said, and for six days women
Fluttered in the camps of enemies
When the spirits of their men blew out.

At the front of the lodge of his chief
He threw down forty scalps, and there were
Twelve boys and young women
Brought back tied up.

I give you your choice if you will speak,
He said to his chief. Tell them that I
Am a brave one. Tell them to bury this mocking.
The chief said, Now let all those words
Lie in the mouth. But remember the joke.

Tshizunhaukau

A Winnebago Warrior
July 1817

Not born for the chase but a brave
Of valor, he was a one who kept
The line between. There was much woman
With the man.

          When he fell
From the high tree, he was six:
His brain slipped in the skull
And he left himself for a while.

He learned enough then to take time.
He found how to heal others—
How to let them float in.

There were voices to teach him:
Remember the deer when you sleep,
When they run.

Speak when you are good for the work.
Wait for the father of the doe
In the thicket.

He grew, and soon a nervous wife
Begged him to conjure a baby
To move her womb.

          Old men,
Bent from grudge-in-the-throat,
Came with dry, white scars

To cool in his shadow.
Many called him Young Poultice-Hand
For in his palm was fire

They would not see. Medicine-men
Loved him, and told him that their art
Was too far up for him to touch.

One day he entered the forest to take
A week's fast. When he returned he walked
An oak staff, notched deep. He told of

Knife visions, and of deer spirits
That scratched with sharp black horns
To make great magic on living wood.

Their marks showed where the moon would sleep
And days that lightning could not bite.
One end was cut for all the yellow stars
No one else saw.

          And when he died
Two snow-white bucks entered the lodge of death,
Caught up the staff on their shining racks,
And cantered up the air to heaven.

Red Jacket

reads a stone
July 1782

As the drinking hummingbird
And the midwinter dancer
I am of the world—not on it.

As the red-mantled woodpecker
And the black-dappled woodpecker
My alarums ring throughout the forest.

Tustennuggee Emathla
A Creek Chief
April 1811

From the cradle, his implements were ever
For war. A gourd rattle, clubbed in his fist,
Bruised the stale air of the lodge:
His cries had battle cadencings
And alarmed his sleeping father, whose hands,
Bound up from darkness, reached every night
For his lance.

            He was of eighteen years
When the Creeks took Fort Mimms.
He was not asked to go with warriors:
They did not want young men.
So he stole out a morning's march
And threaded along the trees, a secret
From the rest of the party.

The carnage was methodical, intense.
No one who was White and who took breath
Was suffered to live. They saw him
Stepping over corpses with dry hands
Locked behind his back. His careful eyes
Ran blood back to each wound.

When he grew a man he gave his strength
To General Jessup, who promised to save his farm
When the rest were transported out of their land.
He fought. He came home to ashes
And a stripped field. Then he was told
How four of his children sank and drowned
With the rotting **Monmouth** as it ferried them
Across the deep, slow river to exile,
Away from muskets and their shining teeth.

Nesouaquoit

A Fox Chief
August 1831

In guarded health and falling deaf, the Lance
Gave away his title in a creaking voice
To his best and eldest son, the Bear
Who Dwells In The High Forks Of Trees.
Bear swore a careful oath: his father had remembered
A dusty annuity that the Whites had promised
Twenty years before, now all tarnished
With arrears, interest.

                        I tell you,
Said old Lance, the Great One of Waussee-Town,
Ah, that one, he is benevolent and strong,
And in his heart are many kindnesses
That burden. He is forgetful; this I understand.
Maybe he is old and dull, like me.
But go there soon; ask for it; he is a fair one;
He will give it.

                        To make that journey,
Bear needed money, and a White man
From Saint Louis made it business.
I'll pay your way to Washington and back,
Said he, and give you meals, hotels,
Whatever else you'll need. And what I want
Is three and one-half boxes full
Of silver—that's a thousand to a box.
Maybe you can sell some skins.

At Washington the Bear was audited
By two gaunt under-secretaries whose pens
Crackled as they spoke. The President, they said,
Is indisposed. He has catarrh. He is regretful
Such incidents occur. Bear hurred home:
His papers, waxed and ribboned, rode in leather.

Now carcasses of beaver, heavy with blackflies,

Rot wide-eyed as vultures fall to eat,
And all the lakes around La Platte
Are running from their edges. Game
Mires along the shore. Fish bloat,
And the center of the water is black.

Red Jacket

to his daughters
November 1792

When we hunted, hunger ran beside us.
We ran in silence, and our stomachs
Burned within to give us power.
We grew the hair-face; we were Wolf;
We were Catamount; we caught
The scent of deer in the wind's hair
And ran them down fainting, light-footed,
Desperate, and when we bloodied them
The sky went red.

We rejoiced in the entrail-gift
That spilled when we cut: we dipped out
The smoking liver, broken from running,
With eager hands. And back at camp
Women fell to work with flint and knife,
And we boiled venison in great kettles,
And we ate until we slept, and we dreamed
Deer-spirits, and we thanked deer-spirits
As we rose from our bodies in dreaming.

I tell you I think on those days
And blacken my heart. Now the White man
Trades us out of the hunt.
He leads us down to a place of fences.
He shows us the way of pens and stables.
Now we rise from warm blankets, and food
Bares the throat to us at sunrise,
And our knives shine from much use,
And I am hungered to my soul's deep.

Hayne Hudjihini

The Eagle of Delight:
An Oto Woman
August 1821

At the first sight of the City of the Father
She clapped her hands, and her laughter
Made the sound of many quail
Startled by foxes.

                She said to her husband:
I will sit at his side to see him eat.
I will look at the dresses of his women,
And I will tell him all my heart has.

When I give him my present I will
Take his hand and make the little kneel
That White women do for all their great men.

At the brass threshold to the polished marble floor
She slipped off her moccasins, and began to wade
Inside. Her husband said:

Do not raise your garment. Do not show
Your limbs to these men. This water
Is false. It is the glass that these men walk upon.

She became a pretty center for concern:
One lady gave a corset. Another gave pomade
For her braided hair. Their husbands thought on her

Through brandy and cigars. When she met Monroe
She curtsied and kept silent and her eyes
Never left his cravat. She presented the tobaccopouch
That she had beaded.

                At the dinner she ate
And fainted away: she awoke in a cloud
Of ammonia and roses. Tell the Father I have seen,
She said, and all that I have seen is true:
Now my spirit wants to leave me, and go home.

Wabishkeepenas

A Chippewa Warrior
July 1826

The Great Rock of Copper, as pure as
Minted silver, veined with serpentine and
Spar, was the brightest manitou
At Fond du Lac. It lay in the water
Of a nearby river and weighed two tons:
And this was after many pieces
Had been carried away for ceremony.

The young White nation heard of it
And thought it a sign. A careful boat
Was sent out, for each rumor
Had been written down. But the Chippewa
Made silence. Then Chief Image-In-The-Stone
Said, Someone tell the White man what he needs.
Someone tell him how to go there. Our rock
Is God's thumb maybe. Maybe it is not.
I tell you Whites will pay us for that Rock.
They will pay to see if there is more.

Wabishkeepenas said, that was a holy place
Before you spoke those words. You are high
Among our men, and what you say
Goes walking. I have seen the Rock
Three times, and each of the three times
My guts were made cold. But now
It is dead. I will take the Whites to it.

The next day heavy weather
Cut up lake water. Many Chippewa
Lined the shore to throw stones.
The boats made wide circles.
High winds took maps to heaven.
Wabishkeepenas said, I am drunken
From all this evil. All rivers
Are the same river and my eyes
Carry nothing I remember. My hands
Hurt like old hands. I know nothing.

He came home and no one spoke to him.
His woman spat in his face. His children
Began to cough blood. His lodge
Fell to the rot. All deer
Knew when he hungered. All rabbits
Jumped over his snares. For six years
He dug roots and ate berries.

Then McKenney, the White Eagle, came
Through Fond du Lac. He wished to see the Rock
And was not afraid. Wabishkeepenas,
Thin and naked, gave him counsel,
Saying, Let the Eagle guard his tongue:
God hates a proud man. No boat
Can carry off the Rock and no chief
Can kill it. Its arms are long.
It has reached through my ribs. I am dead
Walking. Take me with you.

Clasp-Of-Silver

to her daughter
July 1796

One day in the late life of spring, thy Father
Reveled in the blooming sweetgrass while the sun
Was brash. All the trees were fat. He said,
Wife, I shall go from here to walk
Within the fullness of this season.

As the sun was setting, thy Father returned.
His steps furrowed the ground; his neck
Was bent for winter wind; his face
Was lined and stained; his proud mouth
Was narrow-held—the lips were white.

Woman, he said, I have tried to walk.
But whenever I got to stride, and felt blood
Race in my thighs, I came to a fence
Split from the broken meat of trees,
Stacked like feast-game.

Many times did I meet these corpses;
Many times did I turn away. I went eastward
And thought on the place where life comes,
But death lay everywhere: never could I
Walk my spirit to the sun's face.

Then a black cloud clutched my throat
And I sat down on a rock, and wept:
The deer, who vault those rotting logs
As if they were shadow and dreaming,
Will know my sorrow as they lick my tears.

Washinggusaba
An Omahas Chief
1720 - 1800

Piked in ranks to the entrance of his lodge
Were eyeless heads of enemies,
And as flesh shrank on tall poles
And jaws dropped in tall grass,
Black Crow would tell his people

That agony wracks the disobedient
Even to the Other River, and that as long
As heads are trophies, the Beyond
Would hear wailing. He was smooth and oily,
And whosoever chaffed him at Council

Would die in this manner: first
The tongue and the sockets for the teeth
Would burn with no smoke. Then
The stomach and the pipe below
Would empty of blood and cleave

To the spine. Black Crow was fat,
And his hands never left the pouch
Of his medicine. He said God
Had given him his yellow medicine
To be a stiff rod to those that fell

Beneath his rule. He was eighty when he died.
He grew too weak to walk and was carried.
His hair fell from his head. Dark lines
Rose in his nails. His fine burial-blanket
Was heavy with a hundred beaded suns.

Notchimine

An Ioway Chief
August 1831

War is when murder is paid.
When one man falls to sickness
And rips out the spirit of another,
That dead man walks and no one sees;
He speaks and no one hears him,
Lifts the head to him. Revenge

Is high mercy, but the Whites
Cannot understand. They tell us
That a killing for a killing is wrong
In God's eye. Once I spoke to God
About this matter and He said
Whites are fools:

Their cities are crowded with dead men
Shouting, and at night
When their lapdogs wheeze in terror
And the rooms for their beds go cold,
They sleep on,
And lost ones trouble their dreams.

Someone must die to give them peace.
When our half-chief was caught and clubbed
By a band of Sioux, we made a war
On the Sioux: in that way
Our Brother could travel across
The Great River and drink of the water

Where the hunt never ends.
Before we left to kill, we took a deer
And feasted, and then we dreamed.
God showed the two prisoners
I would take. When I woke I made oaths
So it had to be done.

Three days out we came upon the Sioux.
I caught up a woman and a dying man
Who had taken a ball from a musket.
As the spirit passed from his forehead
Our murdered Brother, waiting ten steps
Back of us, nodded. Then they were gone.

Red Jacket to Clasp-Of-Silver
May 1797

This night a high call writhes in air
As unseen smoke: there is a woman
Who is wanted. There is a man who keeps me awake.

Wife, it makes me laugh, this young man
Of the elderberry flute who whistles me
Out of my sleep, who rouses a man

Named He-Who-Keeps-Them-Awake
As token of vigilance. My eyes open
For an old song from this man-of-spring.

What desperate times, those night raids
Into the women! I and my Brothers
Would languish from our heat in the forest

With bold talk of the girls we wanted,
And where we might lurk to meet them,
And whether they were comely in the blanket.

Those were brave days. We waited near lodges
And places for water-drawing.
We earned many blows and many sharp words

From many mothers, and the pretty daughters
Blushed for us—they covered their laughter,
And young shame whipped us hard.

Turn to me, good woman, for that song
Enters my loins. Come close.
Think my former name, the name

First given me, for the flute makes me
Always-Ready and this night
Is the night of a young man. I long for you.

I grow heavy. Now Brother Owl glides quietly
To his mate. Now Grandmother Moon draws clouds
Close about her. Come under my blanket.

Monkaushka

A Sioux Chief
September 1799

The young make weary servants: their elders
Press a menial existence upon them
With the admonition that strong character
Is the fruit of drudgery. Monkaushka,

Skinny pot-boy, sullen horse-holder,
Heard that a White man, far from home,
Vulnerable, foreign, unavengeable,
Fell from a slight that was never intended.

Much glory runs in the steaming blood
Shed for other blood: Many men give
The audacious a path upward and smile
Watching them walk it. Said he,

I am willing to avenge the brave White man
Who was basely struck down. I claim
Solemn duty. I will be Father or Brother
Or Son for I make his flesh mine.

The other children laughed. That evening
He ran along his trail with a rusty axe,
And when he took an Ioway head and arm
By five uncertain strokes, Council sat him
Near the way in.

Caa-Tou-See

An Ojibway Warrior
June 1824

In first light, before the sun rises,
When mist clings to thick rushes
At the shore of the chilly lake,

Caa-Tou-See, kneeling his canoe,
Listens to walking herons while he
Threads sunken trees. No wind blows.

He is drawn to large, mossy fish
That hover in shore-water
And cast out circles as they brush reeds.

His fish-spear carries a horseshoe-nail
Driven in the tip. At each side
Barbs of willow spread to embrace.

The fish are gathered behind the gills
And lie quietly in their great casket
Of birch. Caa-Tou-See drifts

Into the dawn, thinking of his fishing,
And the favored ornaments for his person,
And the way they glint when he is dancing.

Red Jacket

to his daughters
September 1799

When White men came in their great boats
Of oak and canvas, they were Brothers
Whom we fed and taught. To us they gave
Axeheads and kettles of iron, and in return
We let them thrive on a small patch of land
To grow food. Sharing was, those days:
War-hands were covered and there was feasting.

Then Evil One threw dirt in their faces
Making them blind for a while. And when
They knelt by a river to bathe their eyes,
Evil One crouched to whisper, saying,
Thou hast tasted and drank of the land:
Art thou not hungry? Then the Whites stood up,
And their heads were wet, and they were greedy.

They brought forth money and gave it us.
We sold away the land of our fathers.
They brought forth cards and gave them us.
We gambled away our money and honor.
They brought forth rum and gave it us.
We howled like wolves and struck each other.
And then they brought forth a rotten bone:
Pestilence choked us as we slept.

O daughters, my raven's-wing-haired ones,
My mothers of warriors, my weavers of sweet grasses,
On spring nights when no frog sings and Owl trembles,
Thou wilt hear, with the true ear of spirit
A laugh that is high, lilting. Be not deceived,
For it is the voice of Evil One,
Mocking the ashes of our Good Great League.

Wakechai

A Sauki Chief
April 1832

A wise and safe counsel, the Eagle
Who Crouches spoke only
To balance. His best eye

Would fix on the one who was speaking
While the other cut deep in his shadow.
He was a foe to all rash men.

But when he started dying, he caught
A fever from the musty swamp:
Then a voice came into him

Saying, O thou brave Eagle, rise
From thy pallet of infirmity and age;
Open thy wings of copper and brass.

That river of the many many smooth white stones
Is a palace of spirits. Here dwell I.
Come. Embrace me. I will take

All thy fevers up from thee, and I will
Revive all the graces of thy first good days:
Then I will show my face to thee.

Burning, thirsty, taut, he stood up
And told his three wives to dress him
In his best garment, and his silver

Ear-pieces, and his studded leather
Gorget, and his long wooden pipe
With the bowl of red catlinite.

Trembling on his staff, he limped down
To the deepest bend. He drew breath
And cast himself in. At the bottom

He saw only dark. He heard nothing
But the rushing of chilly water.
He came to the top for air

And went down again. His clenched eyes
Throbbed yellow and white. His pipe
Struck a gray boulder and cracked.

Then a spirit took him by his hair
And slowly swam for shore. Terror
Gave him quiet while his palsied face

Stared upward, unmoving, at the sun.

Red Jacket

solus
August 1801

Across the horizon a lone crow
Works against wind: his wings creak.
His eyes are wide for situations.

This is a wise crow: alone
Of his Brothers he is scout
And prophet. He would prefer

An owl, out in the day light,
As reason to call to Brothers,
A chance to conjure old hatred.

If he shouts a certain way
Others will come, also shouting,
Circling the owl with keen beaks

And dirty yellow feet.
When few crows come, they die:
Often there are many many crows.

I think this day will darken
By crows. This night my dreams
Will be yellow and black.

Last night dream-crows became
Pieces of an old black pot.
Then they rose to rejoin

In air: yellow beaks
And yellow feet bristled
From that black cloud

And yellow eyes led it
As it searched out owls.
That was a terrible dream

To have. A terrible dream.
This is the magic I want:
I want a good peace for crows

And for owls. I want
Black pots painted red, white.
I want three nights sleep

As a flat gray stone. Then
My jaw will not make
My teeth grate. Then

My throat will not rattle.
Then my wife will see morning
With a gentle tongue.

Okeemakeequid

A Chippewa Chief
August 19, 1825

At the White man's insistence,
The Sioux and Chippewa, long at variance,
Sat together at Prairie du Chien
With empty hands.

One Sioux chief wore a mantle
From the face of a deer: it burned
On red cloth. From his headdress
Two shining black horns

Thrust up at his temples. Four feathers
Were caught between them. He wore
A tunic of purple and gold. His leggings
Were purple and gold.

Throughout the long councils, during
The good speeches, this chief carried
His head upright: his dark eyes
Fought off gazes.

Next the high fire, Okeemakeequid
Stared with lips open:
Yellow light fell on gold; his breath
Trembled; he stammered.

Okeemakeequid went to him, saying,
Brother, now there is peace where we carried
Hatred; now the rage of our people
Passes in smoke.

Brother, let there be peace. I pledge
A token between us: let us trade garments
With the other. Let us do this
For He The Unknown.

Okeemakeequid put on this clothing
And felt the pressure of the mantle

And the way dark horns
Weighted his head.

His eyes became narrow.
He made long strides and watched
His shadow. His backbone
Gave noises.

Then the Sioux said, Ah, Brother,
Tell me these garments are
Truly great wealth. Tell me the women
Will cry you

To the comfort of their bodies.
You must be happy. You must
Tell me you are happy. Okeemakeequid said,
Oh my Brother,

I am the eagle who struts on crags
For his mate. I am the rutting stag
Wakened by dawn, hungry
For many does.

The Sioux looked inside him, saying,
Brother, four feathers rise like manhood
From the crest of that headdress.
When you touch them

Remember: each one is a scalp
I have torn from your people. Remember:
I have made this strong vengeance
On the day of your peace!

Red Jacket To
Reverend Cram
July 1805

Brother, I have listened to your stories.
I have passed them through my mind. I have
Turned my eyes close upon your face—to me
Each motion of your lips is a white bead
On message strings, caught in the fist of a runner.

You say your Jesus is God's son:
If your god is truly God, he needs no child
To share that power. Have you not said God
Walks all places, and his arms will not break,
And his breath quickens the dead, and his eyes

Peer into the heart? Tell me—what strong man
Needs sons to stand with him? You say God
Gave this son to the world of men,
Who killed him with torture and nails.
Tell me—what father, knowing, thrusts a son

At certain death? If this is true,
Then God a White man is, for all men know
Whites cuff their young for petty wrongs
Yet stroke the dogs beside their feet:
This is a thing we do not understand.

Brother, you have heard old stories of torture
And long days of great pain: when such men died
They made part of our League. Their blood
Became our blood; their agony our strength.
They never cried out, and that gave magic.

Now you ask us to take up the Jesus, though we
Never tortured him, though he twice cried out
To the ghost you call his father. My brother,
Listen: I think you are too eager to believe.
You give too much to one who was merely wise.

Continue to listen: White men think too much.
White men live the Jesus-word too little.
They make their god a wicked father.
They make their god a fool, and if you speak
To such a one, you are a fool as well.

McIntosh

A Creek Chief
May 1, 1825

Five times over there were cessions
To Georgia, and each marked paper
Made the land vanish. The Creeks vowed
There would be no more: no one chief
Would ever hold that power.

The Commissioners were eager. Two of their number
Came to McIntosh, saying, Meet us
At Indian Springs; press your hand once more
Against our papers, sell us land.
Bring down your great chiefs soon;

Bring down your best men. Bring down
Three thousand, and we will give out
One hundred boxes of our silver, and we
Will carry you to new places
Across the Great River, and we will

Preserve you from the wrath of your people,
And stand as a fence of iron. Call out
In a high pitch; air this matter
With dignity. Our Good Great Father
Must think on this hard: work quickly.

But there was no time to call
The three thousand, and McIntosh found but fifty
To assent and to witness: only thirteen chiefs
Of small importance, save for himself
And Etomie Tustennuggee.

After this bad treaty, thick papers
Rode to Washington on lathered horses,
And in twenty days and five days
Great Father and all his best men
Spoke over them, finding them suitable.

Soon the Nation of Creeks

Was consumed with anger and vengeance:
They cried out to Menawa, the Great Warrior,
Saying, Take an hundred of men,
Go to the place of the McIntosh,

Slay every man who spoke us unlawfully.
Slay the son of McIntosh,
Who stood behind his father with the pen
Of White men. Slay Etomie Tustennuggee,
For he is a fool at a high station.

When the days past that treachery
Were seventy and seven, Great Warrior
Stood before the house of McIntosh:
He stood with an hundred of men
Who bore muskets and fat torches.

Menawa threw out a strong voice:
This McIntosh, whose father was White,
Whose musket was raised with White muskets
At Autossee, must die. He broke a law
He helped to utter. He has taken up

With gamblers who wager with land
At their places of drinking,
Who raise axes at the toss of cards.
Let the Whites who are in this house
Come forward—no harm will be given.

Then the Whites who were in that house
Ran out the door as startled magpies:
The Creeks stood aside to let them
Take to the forest. And this is how
Chilly McIntosh, the wicked son, escaped,

For he was light of skin,
Lighter than his father.
Menawa raised his arm and brought it down,
And many torches fell within that house
Through windows of oiled paper.

Soon those traitors burst through fire
With their heads in blankets. Muskets

Thudded and smoked. McIntosh was blown back
To his threshold, and heavy ball
Tore an arm from the shoulderbone,

And carried away his jaw and cheek,
And crushed an eye in the skull,
And pierced his lungs—he bled in front
And from the back. Menawa said,
Now this one will die quickly.

Then Etomie Tustennuggee stood erect
And threw off the blanket: musketfire
Rent his bowels and his belly. He fell
In his entrails; he was left to die slowly;
The Creeks made a ring to watch him.

Red Jacket

solus
January 1807

For three days snow has given flesh
To air. Men and women walk through it
And disappear. Often I see Brothers
Who have gone, and when I go to them
They are someone else.

Tell me, Spirit, why this winter
Turns my brain. Tell me, Spirit,
Why my heart grows damp
By the fire, at the lap
Of my wife.

No face is sure. Snow
Covers gametracks, makes the forest
Still, as if before battle. My ears
Ring from quiet. Not even children
Can break it.

Here comes a Brother, who fell
By the clubs of enemies, whose skull
Was caved in when we were young.
I know he is dead, yet my heart races
And my arms reach to him.

Red Jacket

to his kinsmen
July 4, 1815

This is a remembrance day. The Whites
Wash their city with beer and rum;
Muskets speak with cannon; bright cloth
Marks air, and Father England
Is called a fool by children.

Brothers! We sit in torn blankets
And scratch the ground for food.
Brothers! Game has fled to the west;
The racks empty of meat; our land
Is no greater than the longhouse-border.

The Whites love Liberty. Her face
Shines out from their silver and gold;
Her name is uttered in the high voice;
She stands in brass atop great houses;
Strong men move in her shadow.

Brothers! She is a dull woman
Whose children walk without counsel:
No good stories fall from her mouth.
Brothers! She is a timid widow
Who cannot shame her sons and daughters.

Brothers, this woman has a son
Who is called Freedom. Fear this man,
For he steals with paper and whiskey,
And he bruises the earth with iron shoes:
I name him No-Man-Punishes-Me.

Neamathla

A Seminole Chief
February 1824

By the sixth article of the Treaty of Moultrie Creek, in the territory of Florida, it was provided that the sum of one thousand dollars per annum, for twenty years, should be supplied by the United States to the support of a school at the Florida agency for the education of the children of the Indians. In carrying the provisions of this treaty into effect, the commissioner for Indian affairs at Washington received no information for some time touching that one for the establishment of the school, and supposed it to have been overlooked. The delicate office of communicating this decision to the Governor of Florida was confided to Neamathla . . . .

James Hall, 1836

Father, listen: I will tell you how
The Great and Good Spirit caused Man to be,
To walk upon this earth. I will tell how
He sent tools and weapons for their hands,
To fight, to live. In First Times,
After he had circled his power
To form room for lesser spirits,
He knew being alone: He wished for men
To receive his compassion.

Then
The Master of Life touched his pipestem
To cold clay, saying, Man will We make,
And earth rose and stood before him.
Yoh! It was White Man! Then the Good Spirit
Felt a sorrow, for White Man was weak,
And his flesh was bloodless and pale
As a small winter moon. But Spirit
Had great pity—he did not cast him
Back in the earth.

Now Spirit
Is strong in thought: he wanted a man
To please him, so he touched
Rich loam in pine forests, saying,

Make Man We will, and yoh!
Black Man was before him! His body
Was muscled, shining like earth's blood
That bubbles in places of healing. But Spirit
Frowned, and told him, Stand aside: I must
Lay my calumet again to earth.

And then
He touched sacred hills where
Red pipestone crops out from rock,
Saying, We will make Man, and yoh!
Red Man sprang up before him:
His skin was the color of his blood;
His blood was the color of the stone.
Then the Master of Life placed his long pipe
In his arm's crook, and grew satisfied.

Father, you must know that the Great and Good
Looked down on these men: he saw
Much trouble. Their hands were empty.
They wore nothing for struggle. So Spirit sent
Three large boxes to them. They floated down
Like feathers of sparrows when kites
Graze them. Spirit said, White Man,
I pity you, and I made you first. Choose:
Look in each box; choose.

White Man
Lifted all lids, looked, thought. He chose
A box filled with measuring chains and rods,
Compasses and clean paper. These
Are the tools he has used ever since.
Then Spirit said, Black Man, I made you next
But I do not like you. Stand aside:
Let Red Man, whom I love greatly,
Whose color is holy stone, choose the way
He will wrestle the world.

Red Man said,
O Spirit, I choose this box
That is shining with pipes of copper,
And iron traps and steel hatchets,

46

And lances trimmed in brass and feathers.
Then Spirit laughed aloud, and his laugh
Trembled rivers. O Red Child, he said,
You have chosen good days; your kinsmen
Will burnish your memory; you are a mirror
For my sun.

       Then the Spirit Of All Spirits
Said, Black Man, the last of these boxes
Leave I to you. Use it well; live.
And Black Man opened the box
And found oaken pails to carry water,
And a shining axe to clear new ground,
And a long, thick whip to drive oxen.
This is why Black Man labors hard
For White Man, for Red Man:
Father, you know it has been this way
For every day the two of us have seen.

Father, we are people of many stories: you
Are White and Christian and have but one story
And you make it a hard rule. That you are so
Is a difference. You are kind when you offer
Money for a place to tell your story. But Spirit
Made us different. He is content with all his work,
And so are we.

Red Jacket

solus
Christmas Day, 1824

This day my wife pounds corn: the strokes
Of the wooden mortar flash the brass cross
She wears between old breasts, heavy
With the memory of milk.

The Christians bustle and grin. My wife
Smiles, for the wooden church of the Whites
Will hold her soon in its maw: tonight
She will chant English, she will bear candles.

All this comes from her vision. This
Is the fashion in which she honors it,
And I remain her husband, and my dignity
Is dust on the graves of pretty daughters.

Woman, all my curses were in vain.
The faces of Whites pierce my sleep.
A captive god shimmers at the throats
Of our little children.

No White who vows the Jesus words,
No Quaker, No Black-Coat,
No earnest-hearted young White man
With his clever tongue, with his pitted face,

Will rise above himself to keep the promise.
Today such words are snow.
Today the Christians reach to grasp,
And chilly water courses down their arms.

Red Jacket

solus
March 1825

Though the house is dark, a storm
Hatchets my eyes: I see light
When I want blindness. Fists of thunder
Rattle low hills: men of the valley
Are afraid, and I am old. I am
An old black stone.

              Take me now, thou
Death-That-Forks, thou Sunder-The-Rock:
I feel thee through wood walls,
And the nails in my White house ring
From your maul of noise. My ears
Are dull, yet I hear your hand's clap
Deep in my eye-sockets.
The bones of my face ache. The air
Is deathly sweet.

             This storm is sharp.
I start many times. I think on my daughters
Who are gone. I have no name.
I am a louse in Spirit's hair.
I will be plucked out, thumbnail-cracked,
Thrown to the ground to rot.

Metea

A Potawatomie Chief
ob. 1827

Summoned by his people to make speeches
He journeyed to high ceremony
Near the village of White Plains.
There council was with Whites:
They were vague, insistent. Metea
Kept erect—their shaded words
Made him listen with his nerves.
He held his face with care.
His spine began to hurt. Water and salt
Matted the back of his head.

When the fires were smothered with earth
He said to a trader, I wish
A good frolic; I must rest now
In laughter; I will have friends by me.
I slip off my good robe. My rank
Will I hide in a bundle.
Trader gave him whiskey in a green glass
The size of a fist. He drank.
He fell inward and bitter, saying, Trader,
Pour me out whiskey for I am thirsty.

Metea reeled the village with his glass.
The sun whirled his eyes; the wind
Staggered him and made him fall down.
He came to a door on the street
Where there were small brown bottles
With stoppers of frosted crystal. He cried,
There is much due me. I will drink.
He snatched a bottle from the shelf.
He bared teeth and drank it off.

He died outside. He lay dusty in the street
When White men nudged him with their boots
And children tapped him with their sticks.
Someone shouted for a wagon, and a canvas
To hide him from the eyes of women.

The apothecary, who had been rattled,
Threatened to bill the village council
For thirty drams of aqua fortis.

Totapia

A Choctaw Woman
ob. 1829

Her youngest son was a man of rage:
He slew an old one who had no eyes,
Whose tongue was sharp at puppies.
For this a clan cried out for his blood,
And he was taken by kinsmen for vengeance.

On the day set aside for his death
His people circled him. Chiefs
Called for good weapons to lay
By his feet. Chiefs called out the names
Of those that would kill him.

His mother slipped through warriors
To stand by his side. She faced her chiefs,
Saying, Brothers, listen: this man has a woman
And two small children. When he dies,
They hunger. Continue to listen:

My breasts are dry. My womb
Is rough and dead. Let the grave for my son
Hold me, for I am an old shirt
That no one will trade for. I say now
I will stand in that place my son is.

The chiefs assented, and Totapia
Walked to the house of Mrs. Tyler, whose man
Had a large farm. She sat in the parlor
Where a tall clock spun, and a marmalade cat
Dozed against her skirt.

Mrs. Tyler dabbed her eyes, saying, Jenny,
I have heard your son is to die:
What can I do to help you in your hour
Of great sorrow, for you are a friend
And have been a good worker

When the crops have come in, and the kitchen

Was busy. Totapia said, I wish a strong coffin
And twenty brass nails. I wish a winding-sheet
Of white homespun. Make these to my size,
For my son has my stature.

Mrs. Tyler fetched her sewing basket
And ran a cloth tape from Totapia's head
To the heels of her feet. She said, Jenny,
You shall have what you ask for
In the space of seven days.

At the high point of the seventh day
Totapia stood in the grave, and the open coffin
Was under her feet, and the winding-sheet
Lay folded on the lid. A man
Held a rifle at her throat, and her people

Had made a circle. Then a cry went up:
Mrs. Tyler approaches in her carriage,
And the driver is whipping the horses.
Totapia clutched the rifle and pulled:
The shot tore out her heart.

Five years after, the cowardly son
Took the muzzle of a musket in his teeth.
His death was awkward: the rotten stick
Broke twice before the hammer fell.
Only his woman mourned.

Red Jacket

to his youngest daughter,
June 1829

Even in death I will be close
To this earth: all her dead sons,
Daughters, walking in clear spirit,

Stay here always, for their love is always
For their brown mother. O daughter,
Thy own mother, when thou wast

Beaded in tears from the small bruises
Of children, would grasp her knife
And press the cool flat of it

On thy hurt: the pain fled
From cold steel and ran
Into her broad, veined hands

And then she shook them out. So it is
With this earth. When great men
Stamp their feet, she trembles,

And when there is pain she will
Draw it away. I have felt her work
In days of trouble, when war was,

When many fought and many died.
Always, after she has moved in healing,
She is well. In these my hurtful, latter days,

I lie with her; I am at peace;
She takes up all my sadnesses:
My grave, though I yet live.

Rantchewaime

An Ioway Woman
ob. 1824

Here, where I am, in the clear air
Of spirit, storytellers are talking
In a long lodge. The fire
Always burns and the men
Are always there. Many times
Have I entered, have I asked them
Their stories. They shut their eyes.
They see days that are long dead and days
Yet to be born—and then they sing.

I ask them of Mahaskah,
The good husband, who married me
And my three sisters who were widowed
In war. When they tell me of his courage,
Of his hands that were open and strong,
Of his enemies who lay bloody
On the plain, I sing with them
And the colors of my spirit brighten
To fire: the stories are now one with me.

They have told me that Mahaskah
Shall be struck down by men
Who have water in their bowels, whose eyes
Are wide in his presence. Elder Sister
Will call them dogs, will call them worse than dogs
In the center of our village. My son
Will be there. They say he will not help
With that killing of vengeance, for he
Will make oaths, he will listen to treaties.

My son, whom I carried as a babe when my horse
Felled me, who thought I was asleep
When I came here. All of my insides
Were broken and I was warm
As blood filled me, as a red stream
Ran down the corner of my mouth.
Then my spirit looked down with no sorrow,

Thinking, O to be a man and to paint that wound
Forevermore upon my face as remembrance.

Tonight there is a ripe moon. I will ask
The storytellers to come outside and sing.
We will face the earth and the moon
Will be behind us. When we sing
There will be much power: then
Mahaskah will fly up in a dream,
And though his eyes be closed
And his ears not remember, he will know
That I have pulled him here.

Philip St. Clair was born in Ohio in 1944. He holds a M.L.S. and a M.A. in English from Kent State University and is completing a M.F.A. in Creative Writing from Bowling Green State University. He has written essays on frontier artist James Otto Lewis and pioneer naturalist Louis Jean Pierre Vieillot; his **Frederic Remington: The American West** was published by Bonanza Books in 1981. His first collection of poetry, **In the Thirty-Nine Steps**, was issued by Shelley's Press in 1980. The libretto of his opera, **Crazy Horse**, is presently being scored by ethnomusicologist Halim El-Dabh.

Ahsahta Press

POETRY OF THE WEST

MODERN

*Norman Macleod, *Selected Poems*
Gwendolen Haste, *Selected Poems*
*Peggy Pond Church, *New & Selected Poems*
Haniel Long, *My Seasons*
H. L. Davis, *Selected Poems*
*Hildegarde Flanner, *The Hearkening Eye*
Genevieve Taggard, *To the Natural World*
Hazel Hall, *Selected Poems*
Women Poets of the West: An Anthology
*Thomas Hornsby Ferril, *Anvil of Roses*
*Judson Crews, *The Clock of Moss*

CONTEMPORARY

*Marnie Walsh, *A Taste of the Knife*
*Robert Krieger, *Headlands, Rising*
Richard Blessing, *Winter Constellations*
*Carolyne Wright, *Stealing the Children*
Charley John Greasybear, *Songs*
*Conger Beasley, Jr., *Over DeSoto's Bones*
*Susan Strayer Deal, *No Moving Parts*
*Gretel Ehrlich, *To Touch the Water*
*Leo Romero, *Agua Negra*
*David Baker, *Laws of the Land*
*Richard Speakes, *Hannah's Travel*
Dixie Partridge, *Deer in the Haystacks*
Philip St. Clair, *At the Tent of Heaven*

*Selections from these volumes, read by their authors, are now available on *The Ahsahta Cassette Sampler*.